STICKER ART WITH BRIAN CLARKE

Poppies

"Art has been the great passion of my life:
a magnificent adventure. I hope this book
sparks your creativity and helps you
to find the joy and magic in art."

HENI Publishing, London

2019

2019

ISBN 978-1-912122-88-2

 A catalogue record for this book is available from the British Library.

Designed by Johanna Armstrong
Printed and bound in Malaysia

FSC
www.fsc.org
MIX
Paper | Supporting responsible forestry
FSC® C101773

3

5

7

9

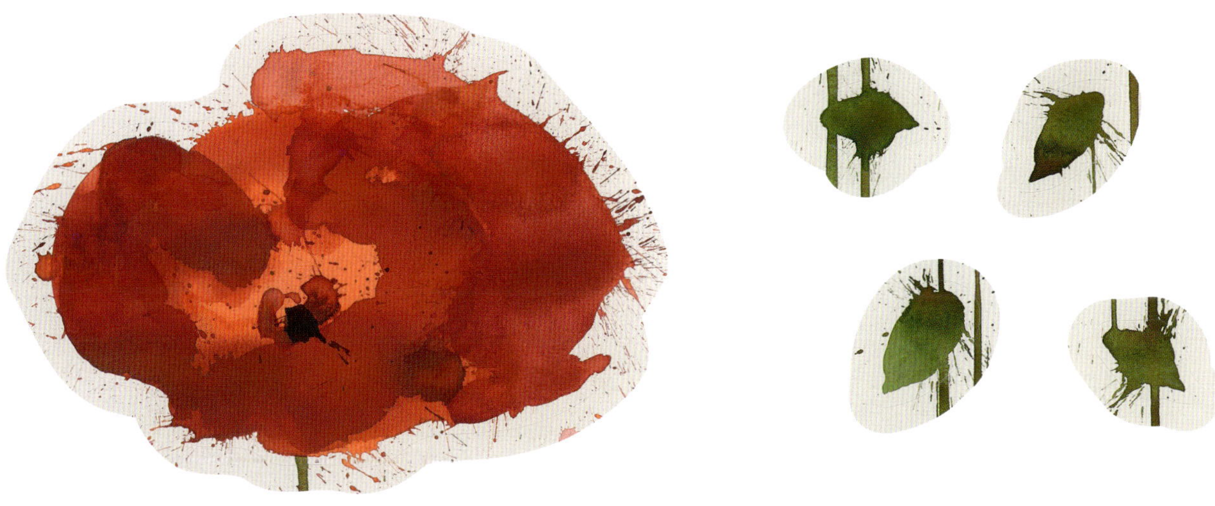

11

13

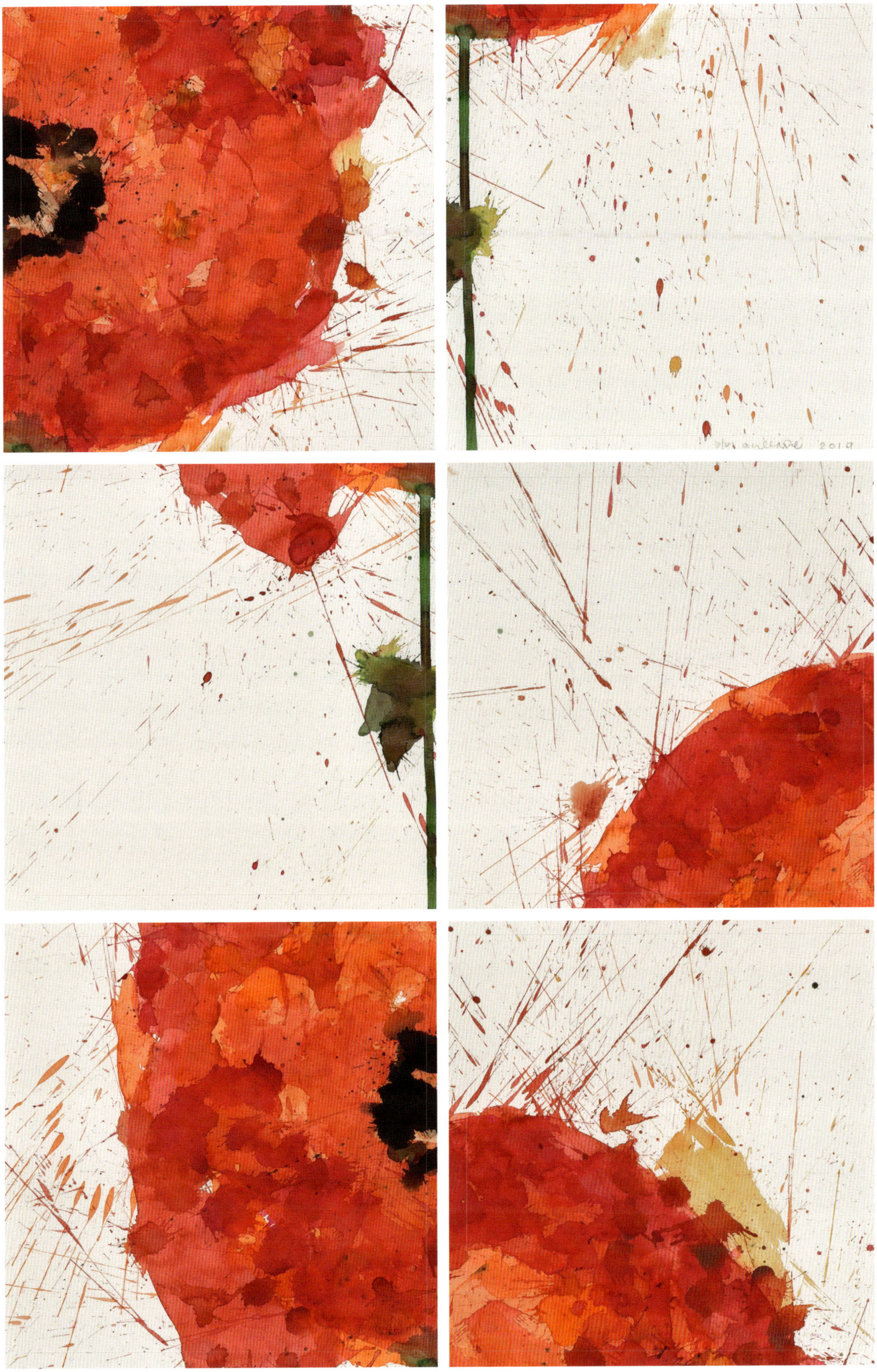

17

19

23

25

27

29